woman | folk

Karan Chambers

Flirtation #32

ò
salò press

This collection copyright © 2025 by Karan Chambers

All rights reserved. No part of this publication may be reproduced, stored in a retrieval system, rebound or transmitted in any form or by any means, electronic, mechanical, photocopying, recording or otherwise, without the prior written permission of the author and publisher. This book is sold subject to the condition that it shall not by way of trade or otherwise be lent, resold, hired out or otherwise circulated without the publisher's prior consent in any form of binding or cover other than that in which it is published.

siren was previously published in *Propel Magazine*; *each-uisge* was previously published in *Gutter Magazine*; *eiocha* & *mnathan-nighe* were previously published in *Clarion*; *here be monsters* was long-listed for the Cheltenham Poetry Competition, 2023; *hebridean spring* was previously published in *Anthropocene* and short-listed for the *Black Cat Poetry Competition, 2024*

978-1-917264-02-0

Printed and Bound by 4Edge

Cover layout by Salò Press

Cover image: *Mabon ap Modron* – artwork by Jen Delyth ©1994 www.celticartstudio.com

Typeset by Andrew Hook

Published by:
Salò Press
85 Gertrude Road
Norwich
UK

editorsalòpress@gmail.com
www.salòpress.com

For R, E, & M –
you have made me more myself than I have ever been.

& for Gary, always.

Contents

hebridean spring	1
the fisher queen	2
woman: drowned	3
here be monsters	4
eiocha	5
each-uisge	7
spell for not-being	8
green lady of fyvie	9
woman: buried	10
siren	11
cailleach	12
selkie	14
spell for being	15
mnathan-nighe	16
woman: hanged	17
spell for naming	18
woman: burned	20
witch	21
woman: free	22
goddess prayer	23

hebridean spring

here is land like an upturned fist. darkknuckled. jutting. awkward angles & uncanny places. a stretch. rock & shingle. skerrystruck. between jawopen seas. here are its quiet hollows. its openreach heights. its spiked invitation. here is the gorse. furzespine prickle. brindlecoated. here is the heather. a restless unfolding. lingslung fire. smoulder & tongueflicker. here is a melody. scattering its way through the leaves. softkeyed promise. fertile ground sings to fallow. here are the women. working. & tending. & growing. & raising the bairns. & dreaming of more. here are the men at sea. except when they're not. except when they're shadowstood. landlooming. claiming what's theirs. it's fine if you're willing. want makes flames of us all. but what if you're not? what if your body can't bear another. we've all seen his hands round her ankles. seen submersion in her eyes.   i know how a woman drowns

the fisher queen

i didn't know the right question to ask & so he fished. every day. he contemplated the water, tracking currents & ghosts. out in his stupid little boat while the land withered around us. i sowed & tilled & coaxed the soil, desperate as my efforts bore no growth. i walked the kitchen gardens, knelt in dust & turned its ashy grey, hoping to find dark loam if i just dug deep enough. each time i pulled my fingers dry & grieving from the earth, the dirt fell away like soot. & when i took my basket to the fields for harvest, corn ears drooped before me & i couldn't bring myself to uproot their shrivelled forms. still he fished. when i took my daughter to the woods to forage, hunting berries & seeds like starving birds, we brought home scraps to make a soup that made our bellies twist & gripe. & still he fished. when the grass crisped under the scorching sun, turning sickly ochre before the wildfires raged. he fished. when the bloody flux came, turning our insides out & killing our old folk in its spite. he fished. when our milk dried up & our babes perished at our breasts, wails becoming whimpers before silence. he fished. when my daughter sickened, turning white & pallid, & i begged him on my knees – he left as usual, peeling my fingers from his ankles, rod slung over one shoulder. i held her hand as she wasted with the land around us, folded hands to shoulders, placed the coins & wound the cloth, as i had done for four small forms before her. only then did i walk down to the shore & let the water close over my head.

woman: drowned

silt-tongued, stonepocketed, her body
a riverbed   eroding
its banks. surfacing with pondweed hair,
she is pearleyed, staring, a glossy
reflection   want
untethered. the drift

of mouth   of cheekbones
seawards, lips & lashes
currentstricken   spurred
into confluence

a warning
for all those who never learned
to swim

here be monsters

here is fog like a hand over your mouth. fingers cold as grave dirt. ashscattering. bonestricken. here is mistmizzle. skittering. rainspun skin. spidered with prickling. webwoven omens. [something. cometh]

here is a morning that muffles. all attempts to run. here ground reaches. tangles. bindweed tripping. here is hunger that swallows small things. here is twistedness stirring. clamping gristwrithen jaws. soft derma. barbed incisions. here are bloodied thighs.

[it's the same
for us all child.
wipe away the red]

here is a broken thing. discarded. dishevelled. strings snapped. limbs splayed. waxdoll silence. here is the brume still. cloudheavy. swathe of vast haar snarling.

[rest
your head here child.
the pain will pass]

here is a girl. taught she can always say no.
here is the world.   showing her otherwise

eiocha

before there was time & gods
& men   who thought they knew
everything   there was
her: tideheld, wavecradled. body buoyed
by water. smoothlined,
oceanfaced.   coralreef ribs expanding
with breath from the breadth
of becoming. hair currentstirred
stretching beyond
the limits   of our knowing. & she was
happy.

but in the place   where sea meets
land, she drew too close
to the shore.   surfchurned, dragging
with undertow, she was caught
& pulled & plundered &
left
bruised & marooned.

the tide drew back   spittlespumed
weeping   leaving
sea foam mixed with salt   & bright red sand
from it rose
a white mare still flecked
with blood
& the bitterness of what had been
taken.

& as her new form swelled & surged she
sustained herself with berries found fallen
from branches   determined to
survive even as she brought forth the life
she hadn't chosen   biting the bark of
the trunk of the tree as the child tore
through her   horsethroated screaming
as her equine body was sundered   &
when the babe lay   covered in blood
she saw in its face her own helplessness &
wondered   what the hell do i do now?

each-uisge

here is the moon as a spoon-back. dipped. ready. here is the water. reflected. tea-dark. cup-held. here is the reed-footed bird. lines studied. still. beak held. expectant. here is stirring. under the surface. here the current. the eddy. whirling. folding water. fang-dark. cutting. here is the mane. serpent curved. twisting. here is sclera unhooded. pupils blown. bleeding. into the dark. irises bloated. saturated.
        drip
           drip
              drip
here is the slide. of slick. muscles. chest bared. here is the touch. shiver-spine. here is the pull. the urge. here is the deep. rearing. too close. here am i. spilled milk. seeping. here is the struggle. too late. here is the water. closing. churning. over howling limbs. here is the moon. a witness. grave cold. when has a woman ever been able to change her mind. without punishment.

spell for not-being

he doesn't care that another babe would kill her. that the last one nearly did. all he cares about is that he's got something to shove it into when he comes home reeking of booze & piss & thick animal stink. red meaty hands pawing at her dress. fingers pressing into tender skin until it tears.

the next day, still aching, she binds the little one to her chest, leaves the older ones with her neighbour, & walks the four miles to the witch. she asks for the brew her sister took last year when her man was working away & his brother came around to check she was getting on alright.

the witch is frightening, with teeth so yellow they make her think of freshly churned butter. she's kind enough though, makes the tea without haggling the price, mixes the hellebore with feverfew & tansy. she holds the little one tighter, trying not to think of the love, only the mess of blood that poured from her after his birth, & the blackness she thought would never end. the water boils & the witch mutters words she can't quite catch over the steeping petals. she hands her a tin cup & tells her to drink it down all at once to stop the babe from quickening.

that night, as she lies in her bed, youngest child cradled in her arms, feeling her womb cramp & empty, she dreams of a different life. where husbands aren't monsters & women aren't holes to be buried in.

green lady of fyvie

here are trees like saw-blades. notched. a sky in slices. [SHE NEVER SAW IT COMING] here is fog like barbed wire. teeth. that tangle & tear. here is skin. ripped. organs laid. bare. [THE HEART IS EXPOSED] here is a woman. her own name. unfamiliar. thick-tongued. here is surprise. like a knife. to the throat. hot blood like wings. in the darkness. here is betrayal. here lies a lover in wait. claws tipped. tongue darted. here is love. that was not. love. [THE BODY IS DISMEMBERED] here the husband. sated. oh. it's a cruel day when he takes everything. [THEY STUFFED HER IN THE WALLS] here are cold bricks. owl-stoned. how can a man kill her for being. too much. [SHE WON'T FIGHT NOW] & now. & now. they fuck. in cinder-blocked shadows. listening. to the echo. of her cries. fingernails scraping mortar. [SHE COMES] [SHE COMES BACK] how will you tell your daughters what you've done. or will you silence them too.

woman: buried

don't look					too closely

    at her eyes

                            they have become

a home

    to worms

                             even after death

her body is still

                             giving

siren

here is the night on a pen nib. sabre carved & starkened. cross-hatched stars. abyss. full. of not knowing. of teetering. here is the moon's bright arch. coffee-stain ring of half. remembrance. here is marshland pressing. below a dead-rimmed sky. rabbit-eared tuft. of longing. bless me. for i have. desired. snatched. wanted. greedy-handed. stuffed my mouth so full. i choked. forgot myself. fleeting. here is the world in an ink spill. thickblack. gleaming. spread like faded light. here the water. waits. eager. manuscript of anticipatory. silence. stuck. in soft-drift splendour. it's been years. since last i stood. here. straining. forwards motion. less. here are my fingers. exposed to the air. freezing. startled. by the depths. here is the sound. of stiff-limbed. resignation. knotted. curling upwards. these are follies. delusions. halfsnarled. roots of forgetting. wisped. vaporous. & somewhere. in the not-here. a small word. of recognition.

cailleach

first frost falls   late   this
year
                 cailleach strikes
the ground   hardens
splits
     stone into   slurryspittle

       two   birds
     land
on a frozen fence
     feathers ruffed
   against
the chill   the sky   bruises
above
     throbs   & air
thins
   in numb   lungs

it's hard to catch your breath
with her hand   on your
chest
     this time   of year
           steady
       ground

staggers
    just out of   reach
unsure feet   slipandslide
towards
     the darkening
   a white veil   cast down

shroud   pall   cerement   it's all
              the same.
there's no way   to lift
          when she's   in the roots

selkie

here is the sea in an iris. glassdark. austere. blackblue ripening. a stare. brazen. fearless. here is the shore like a moon-curve. glowing. here is nakedness. saltslicked beauty. here is the gaspvoiced cry clawing. sand spilling fervour of want.   here

lies the sealskin. discarded. unheeded. velvet tipped spread. transformation. here is the slink. of the voyeur. who wants to possess. take it. hide it well. she'll be yours. here the sea. waits always. calling. how long. how long can you keep her?   here

is the house of violation. landlocked. windows blind. vases empty. sea weed rotting in the beds. here is the silence. the arid drift of shingle. here is what looks like love. here are the babes she holds more tightly than she did her skin.

here are the eyes. seadark. danger. reflecting his smile. & the whisper of a tail   disappearing beneath the waves

spell for being

so many times she held the twig dollies, wrapped strands of her hair around their leafy crowns to bind them to her, stitched the red thread to hold the wooden thighs together. trying each time to stem the flow of blood. sometimes it held longer than others. she might make it to the fifth moon, or the sixth, one agonising time it was the seventh before her body betrayed her, the stitching frayed, unravelled. her husband mourned with her, comforted her, cried with her. in the beginning.

but after the fourth loss he hardened. after the fifth he left & found a woman who bred as easily as the cat who whelps her kittens every season. she sees them sometimes, a brood of boisterous bairns in the village square, rollicking & laughing with their father. he lowers his eyes as she passes but she finds she cannot look away.

now she lives alone, apart from the damn cat & her endless offspring. she finds she can't bring herself to drown them. women come to her, drawn by tales from friend or sister or next-door's goodwife, that she casts charms for luck, or love, for fertility (oh, how that one burns), or for their husband to return safe (or not) from sea or hunt. & sometimes they come for the tea made from hellebore & tansy. her hands shake every time she brews it, but the desperate expressions or the marks of violent men steady her to action. children should be wanted.

it's a half-life she lives. of all the spells she ever cast, the only one that never worked was the one to make her babies stay.

mnathan-nighe

here is the world as a scalpel. slicing. edge so sharp. sky flinches. where it presses. here is the temerity of loving. the folly of hope. here it is. all. taken. here they are kneeling at the water's edge. washing. washing. here are their clothes. still stained. with birth's bright blood. here are their fingernails. turned to cairn stones. their restless work. here they are scrubbing. scrubbing.   yet

here you are creeping. closer. closer. here you are. desperate. for knowledge

here are their bodies. remembering. the babes they never held. arms bearing phantom forms. lips crooning lullabies. no one can hear.

here you are. still. closer.

how badly do you want to know who you'll lose? they'll tell you. they will. if only you can endure the taste of shrivelled dugs. milk curdling in the sacs. they'll tell you anything. if they mistake you for their slipped ones. if they think they're holding them. one last time. feeling their nursing mouths. suck. pull. suck. pull. trick them. it's cruel. too cruel.   can you bear the cost?

woman: hanged

all the bones broken
in one hand, fingernails   split
to the beds. a splinter
of light stuck fast to the palms
& a shiver of blooms
rooted deep. ankle-strung,
                         suspended
until cut — blood rushing straight
to the head — it's a long   wait
      'til the ground.

spell for naming

they called us witch. carline. devil's bride. said we consorted with the horned one. desported ourselves at full moon. fornicated at crossroads. they said we were a coven.

they couldn't stand that we lived without a man. women were jealous. their husbands angry. they thought us unnatural. shunned us from their festivals. hurled cruel jibes at us in the street. said we killed babies. bathed in virgins' blood. ate newly-hatched birds straight from the shell.

we laughed at their tales. late at night. limbs splayed. shining with sweat. it was love that drew us together. no fork-tongued satan could bring me the pleasure she did. no snake-hipped lucifer could tempt me to desire like her. she was the only one i would sacrifice my soul for.

we pledged ourselves under the clootie tree. no one to bind our hands but each other. afterwards we sank, honey-limbed, into the soft green below. hawthorn blossoms drifting down. melting like blessings on our skin.

the season was turning when they came for us. their fear become deeper. bestial. a child had died. cursed by our hands. they said. the harvest had failed. bitter cold sudden after a too-warm samhain. a two-headed calf was born. ripping its mother open as she birthed it.a sign of our barren spite. they said.
                        [thou shalt not suffer a witch to live]

dragged by the hair. hauled through the streets. flung in the dark & mouldering dirt. she confessed. to my shame i let her.

they made me watch. she held my gaze to the end. she never cried out. except once. named me beloved with her last breath.

                      [a woman shall surely be put to death]

of all the forbidden things they whispered that we did, they never touched on the truth: it wasn't the devil we worshipped, but each other.

                      [her blood shall be upon me]

woman: burned

we've all see the marks
& blamed them on the devil. all watched
as she's led to the stake, hands tied

& bleeding. all ignored
the signs – accusations, bruises, false confessions
extracted by a man who wants

to destroy. we've all heard his lies & wanted to believe
we'd never swallow them. all looked away
as he takes her voice. uses her up.

& when, finally, the pyre
appears, looming, impossible
to ignore, we've all smelled the tang of singed flesh
& been glad it wasn't us.

we've all seen a woman burn
& not known
how to put out the flames.

witch

here are wings like steeltips. urgent. ringing. a sky too full to answer. hammered feathers. ironwrought claws. beak & beady burnished eyes. *i forged myself in spite*. here is dark like a heart's cage. folded. echoless. filled with foretelling. *they always feared me*. great white pull. fevercoated. drumming. *they said i was too much*. here is the night with its rhythmroil. slinking. oilslickshimmer. moonwater reflection. *too loud. too raw*. here it is. rising. like a tide. *fuck them*. here are opalboned oracles. omens of return. of rapture. *make them look*. no false church of stone & steeple. *away*. here is the true. hazelkirk. eldershrine. fill your arms with its holythroated bloom. openfaced. welcome. *hold myself*. here are the arches. vaulted with flingfingered sprouting. ready. *as i am*. here is she. *here*. a wild emergence. *always*. tracing spaces from ankle to clavicle. ribs to vertebrae. mapping capillaries & veins. *i won't hide*. aorta. atrium. ventricle. thud. thud. thud. *in the dark anymore*. a topography of self.   unearthed

woman: free

here at the edges   you
wait   ocean reaching
for the shore   spray turning
skin to   salt & glitter

one day   you dip   a toe
in sirensong   & it feels
so good   next day
you lower   your whole self

naked   into stinging
surf   & marvel   at the way
it holds you   the way no one
ever has   marvel

at the way water is
a soft   question   pebbled into dark
the way   your own body
has always been

the answer

goddess prayer

when the hunger wakes me   pulls
my famished body to the woods to hunt
with fang & clawbright smiling
talons   when i leave my children
dreaming   in their beds
as the cravings   gnaw my belly down
to nothing & i slip   featherlight
between trees & roots
& twisted dark   find myself
all padding paws & velvet pelt
beneath
a grinning sky   when i   slink
from stove & broom & heavy hearthstone
hold   crimsoncoated
when i beat my wasting hands
fistflamed   on   bark & stone
& unforgiving   ground   until
    wolfweary

                                        i sink

into your lichen forest kiss
deeper
        deeper
                deeper
                          down

beyond the bones
of all the mothers   just like me
buriedbrokenbruised   who knew
the taste   of hotbrightblood
    & of the kill's last

                        sigh

& when   finally   i rest here
                                              belly full
in your catacomb
bless me   for i am   free

glossary

bairn /*beuhn*/
    a scots/northern english word for small child, baby.
cailleach /*kaly-ack*/
    the gaelic crone goddess, who brings the winter.
cairn /*ceuhn*/ stone
    a scots word derived from the gaelic càrn /*karn*/,
    a pile of stones that mark a burial spot
carline /*kar-lin*/
    a scots word for 'old woman,' interchangeable
    with hag, witch, or crone
clootie /*kloo-tee*/ tree
    a tree, often a hawthorn, hung with rags
    (clooties), as offerings and prayers for healing
eiocha /*ayo-kaa*/
    a figure from a (possibly contemporary) creation
    myth, eiocha was a white mare made from sea
    foam. she ate white mistletoe berries and became
    pregnant with cernunnos, the horned god of the
    hunt.
each-uisge /eck-ooshkaa/
    a water spirit closely related to the kelpie, but
    more vicious, it lives in seas and lochs. a shape-
    shifter, it often takes the form of a beautiful man
    to lure female victims into the water, where it
    drags them to the bottom and devours them.
the fisher queen
    the imagined wife of the fisher king, a figure from
    arthurian legend who guards the holy grail. he is
    often depicted fishing as, due to an injury, he is
    unable to tend to his land, which is now barren
    and wasting away.

green lady of fyvie
> thought to be lilias drummond, wife of the lord of fyvie. the tales say she bore four (some tales say five) daughters to her husband, who was desperate for a son. he had an affair with one of her relatives and lilias died – in some tales she wastes away from a broken heart, in others her husband poisons her, and stuffs her corpse into the walls of the castle. she became a green lady, (a ghost) and still wanders the halls of the castle at night.

mnathan-nighe /*mnahuhn-neeyuh*/
> plural of bean-nighe /*ben-neeyuh*/, they are spirits of women who have died in childbirth and are doomed to wash the clothes of those who are about to die, until the day their lives would have ended naturally. the legends say that if you get close enough and suck a bean-nighe's breasts, she will tell you the name of who is about to die.

kirk
> church

selkie
> creatures who shapeshift from seal to human by removing their skin. the legends say that if you capture the skin, the selkie can be coerced into marriage, but they will continue to long for the sea and will return to it if they ever find their skin.

siren
> sometimes referred to as mermaids or *maighdean-mhara* /my-jong vah-reh/, they were believed to bewitch people and lure them into the water to drown.

Karan Chambers (she/her) is a poet, tutor, and former English teacher. She has a degree in Creative Writing from UEA and is studying for an MA in Creative Writing (Poetry) at Royal Holloway. She has poems in *Butcher's Dog, Gutter, London Magazine, Mslexia*, and *Propel*. Karan was awarded Highly Commended in the Cheltenham Poetry Competition (2023), and Runner-Up in the Classical Association Poetry Competition (2024). She lives in Surrey with her husband and three unruly children. This is her first pamphlet.